The Digital

Protecting Yourself Against Privacy Violators and Cyberthreats

Taylor Royce

DEDICATION

To all the unsung heroes in the cybersecurity field, whose tenacious work ensures the security of our digital lives.

To my friends and family, thank you for your constant encouragement and support along this trip.

And this book is for everyone who works to safeguard their security and privacy in the constantly changing digital world.

CONTENTS

ACKNOWLEDGMENTS

The process of writing this book has involved learning, teamwork, and assistance. My sincere thanks goes out to all of the people that helped in this process by lending their knowledge, time, and encouragement.

First of all, I would like to express my gratitude to the researchers and experts in cybersecurity whose ground-breaking work has inspired and informed the material in this book. It is very admirable how committed you are to furthering this field's understanding.

I would also like to thank the editors and reviewers for their insightful comments and ideas. Your astute observations and painstaking attention to detail have greatly raised the caliber of this work.

Your understanding and support, my encouraging network of friends and coworkers, have been a constant source of inspiration. Your appreciation for the significance of my work has motivated and focused me.

Finally, I want to thank all of the readers. This book is motivated by your desire to safeguard the security and privacy of your digital life. With the knowledge and resources in this book, I hope you may successfully and safely navigate the digital world.

We appreciate your contributions, encouragement, and hard work, everyone.

DISCLAIMER

This book, "The Digital Shield: Protecting Yourself Against Privacy Violators and Cyberthreats," contains content that is solely intended for informational and instructional reasons. Despite their best efforts, the author and publisher cannot be held accountable for any inaccuracies or omissions in the information provided, even though they believe it to be accurate and thorough.

It is advised that readers utilize the information in this book as a general reference and seek the opinion of licensed cybersecurity and legal experts for advice unique to their own situation. The techniques and suggestions covered might not be appropriate in all circumstances, and they shouldn't be used in place of expert counsel.

Any liability resulting directly or indirectly from the use or application of any material contained in this book is disclaimed by the author and publisher. The decisions the reader makes about their cybersecurity and privacy policies are entirely their own.

Any websites, goods, services, or businesses listed in this book are not recommended or endorsed in any way. Links or references supplied in this book to third-party content are not under the responsibility of the author or publisher.

By reading this book, the reader consents to release the publisher and author from any liability for any claims, actions, lawsuits, losses, or liabilities resulting from the use of the information included in it.

CHAPTER 1

Overview of Privacy and Cybersecurity

This book explores the crucial nexus between privacy and cybersecurity in the rapidly changing digital world of today. We'll look at the most recent risks, comprehend how hackers are changing their strategies, and provide you with the information and resources you need to use the internet safely and securely.

1.1 The Networked World: Comprehending the Digital Environment

The internet allows a complex web of devices, systems, and services to communicate and interact with one another, forming the digital ecosystem. Smartphones, PCs, servers, cloud services, Internet of Things (IoT) gadgets, and more are all part of this ecosystem. Every element is essential to the creation, transmission, and storage of data.

- **Internet of Things (IoT):** IoT products, such as wearables, smart home appliances, and connected cars, add to the massive volume of data that is shared on a regular basis. These gadgets frequently have weak security features, which leaves them open to hacker intrusions.

- **Cloud Computing:** Cloud services enable businesses and individuals to access and share data remotely by providing scalable resources and storage options. Although useful, this also presents possible security risks in the event that data is not sufficiently safeguarded.

- **Social Media Platforms**: Due to the large volume of personal information published, social media sites like Facebook, Twitter, and LinkedIn both ease communication and information sharing but also present privacy and data security concerns.

- **Enterprise Systems:** To run effectively, businesses depend on intricate IT infrastructures, which include servers, databases, and networking hardware. Keeping these systems safe from online attacks is crucial to ensuring business continuity.

Acknowledging the significance of cybersecurity and privacy requires first having a solid understanding of the digital ecosystem. Our increasing dependence on digital technology raises the possibility of cyberthreats that could jeopardize both our personal and work life.

1.2 Cybersecurity's Significance: Safeguarding Your Information and Resources

Cybersecurity is the discipline of defending programs, networks, and systems from online threats. These assaults typically target sensitive data access, alteration, or destruction, user extortion, or disruption of regular corporate operations.

- **Personal Data Protection:** Cybersecurity safeguards guard against theft and illegal access to personal data, including credit card numbers, social security numbers, and medical records.
- **Financial Security:** Both individuals and companies may suffer large financial losses as a result of cyberattacks. Preventing fraud and financial crimes requires protecting financial transactions and data.

- **Intellectual Property:** Companies need to protect their proprietary data, trademarks, and patents from being taken or imitated by rival businesses.

- **Stability of Operations:** Cyberattacks have the potential to interfere with company operations, resulting in lost productivity, downtime, and reputational harm. Maintaining ongoing corporate operations is ensured by putting strong cybersecurity practices into place.

Investing in cybersecurity involves not only data protection but also asset protection and trust maintenance. Ensuring the safety and integrity of personal and professional digital assets can be achieved by preventing data breaches, financial losses, and reputational damage with a robust cybersecurity posture.

1.3 Demystifying Privacy: Juggling Control and Convenience

In the digital age, maintaining privacy entails knowing how and when to reveal personal information online as well as how it will be used and safeguarded. Retaining privacy requires striking a balance between control and ease.

- **Data Collection:** Organizations gather information via a variety of methods, such as cookies, online forms, and tracking technology. Although this information can improve user experience and offer tailored services, it also raises questions regarding data protection and usage practices.

- **Consent and Transparency:** Information about what data is being gathered and how it will be used must be disclosed to users. Transparency and user trust are reliant on explicit consent forms and privacy policies.

- **Minimization of Data:** Reducing privacy threats can be achieved by gathering only the information that is required and storing it securely. By putting data reduction techniques into practice, it is ensured that no unnecessary personal information is gathered or kept around.

- **User Control:** Giving users the ability to manage their data via opt-out choices, privacy settings, and requests for data deletion aids in protecting their privacy. Giving consumers the means to manage their data increases their confidence and sense of trust in digital services.

In order to maintain control over convenience, privacy policies must be put in place that uphold user rights and facilitate seamless digital interactions. Keeping users' control, permission, and transparency are essential components of protecting privacy in the digital era.

1.4 The Price of Cybercrime: How It Affects People and Businesses

Cybercrime is the term used to describe a variety of malevolent actions, such as ransomware, phishing, identity theft, and hacking. Cybercrime is expensive and has an impact on both people and businesses.

- **Credit Setbacks:** Significant financial losses can result from ransomware attacks, theft, and fraud in the context of cybercrime. While people may be victims of financial fraud and stolen assets, businesses may be subject to significant fines, legal fees, and compensation costs.

- **Damage to Reputation:** Businesses' reputations can be damaged by data breaches and cyberattacks, which can result in a decline in customer loyalty and trust. Reputation repair may be an expensive and time-consuming procedure.

- **Disturbance in Operations:** Cyberattacks have the potential to impair company operations, resulting in lost revenue, downtime, and decreased productivity. Cybercrime can cause people to lose access to important services and personal data.

- **Results for Law and Regulation:** To safeguard the security and privacy of customer data, businesses have to go by a number of laws and guidelines. If you don't, you risk fines, legal trouble, and regulatory repercussions.

Beyond just causing financial losses, cybercrime also has an influence on the general stability and confidence in digital networks. Knowing how much cybercrime costs highlights how crucial it is to put strong cybersecurity safeguards in place to shield people and businesses from its disastrous repercussions.

You can navigate the complicated world of cybersecurity and privacy more skillfully and ensure a safer and more secure digital experience by being aware of these fundamental ideas.

CHAPTER 2

The Threat Environment: Identifying Typical Cyberattacks

To effectively fight against cyberattacks, one must be aware of the many kinds of attacks. The mechanics behind prevalent cyberthreats, as well as their possible effects on people and organizations, are examined in this chapter.

2.1 Malware Mayhem: Ransomware, Worms, Viruses, and More

Malicious software, or malware for short, is created with the intention of interfering with, harming, or gaining illegal access to computer systems. Numerous malware varieties provide serious risks to cybersecurity.

Viruses:
- **Definition:** When a virus is executed, it affixes itself to a valid program or file and spreads to other programs or files.

- **Impact:** May erase or destroy data, interfere with system functionality, and pilfer private information.

- **Prevention:** Update computers and software frequently, stay away from downloading unfamiliar files, and use dependable antivirus software.

Worms:

- **Definition:** A worm is a type of stand-alone malware that spreads to other computers by self-replicating and frequently taking advantage of network flaws.

- **Impact:** Without human intervention, it has the potential to overload networks, waste bandwidth, and create extensive disruption.

- **Prevention:** Put robust network security measures in place, update software frequently, and keep an eye out for strange activity in network traffic.

Ransomware:

- **Definition**: Ransomware is a type of malware that encrypts a victim's data and requests money for the decryption key.

- **Impact:** May cause operational disruption, financial

loss, and data loss.

- **Prevention:** Consistently create backups of your data, employ strong security software, train staff to spot phishing efforts, and stay away from paying ransoms because they don't ensure that your data will be recovered.

Trojan Horses:

- **Definition**: A Trojan masquerades as trustworthy software but, once installed, takes on malevolent functions.
- **Impact:** May open backdoors, pilfer confidential data, and aid in more assaults.
- **Prevention:** Utilize complete security solutions, download software from reputable sources, and keep up with new security risks.

To effectively implement cybersecurity measures and safeguard systems and data from dangerous attacks, it is imperative to have a thorough understanding of the many types of malware.

2.2 Phishing Frenzy: False Emails Trying to Get Personal Data

Phishing is a technique used by hackers to mislead people into disclosing private information, including bank account information and login credentials, through phony emails and messages.

Attackers send phony emails that seem to be from reliable sources in an attempt to fool recipients into clicking on dangerous links or divulging personal information. This technique is known as "email phishing."

Email Phishing:

- **Impact:** May result in unapproved access to systems, financial loss, and identity theft.
- **Prevention:** Use email filtering services, be wary of unsolicited emails, confirm the sender's identity, and stay away from dubious links.

Spear Phishing:

- **Definition:** A focused phishing assault directed at certain people or companies, frequently employing customized data to boost trustworthiness.

- **Impact:** Increased success rate as a result of the focused strategy, resulting in serious data breaches and monetary losses.
- **Prevention:** Use sophisticated email security technologies, multi-factor authentication, and employee education to identify targeted assaults.

Whaling:

- **Definition:** A type of phishing that goes after prominent people like CEOs or senior management.
- **Result:** can cause serious harm to a business, including loss of revenue and damage to its reputation.
- **Prevention:** Provide executives with frequent security training, make use of email verification tools, and enforce stringent access controls.

Smishing and Vishing:

Vishing and smishing are two different types of phishing assaults. Vishing involves phone calls, while smishing involves SMS texts.

- **Impact:** May result in financial fraud and illegal

access to private data.

- **Prevention:** Avoid giving out personal information over the phone or over SMS, be cautious of unwanted calls and messages, and confirm the identity of the caller or sender.

Understanding the many types of phishing is essential to protecting company and personal data from these fraudulent attempts.

2.3 Social Engineering Pitfalls: Capitalizing on Human Emotions

Instead of using technological flaws, social engineering uses psychological manipulation to trick people into doing things or disclosing private information.

Pretexting:
- **Definition:** To entice people to provide private information, attackers invent a situation.
- **Impact:** May result in data and systems being accessed without authorization.
- **Prevention:** Confirm the identity of those asking

private information, train people to spot social engineering techniques, and set up explicit guidelines for exchanging information.

Baiting:

- **Definition:** To trick users into jeopardizing their security, attackers entice them with something of value, such a USB drive or free software.
- **Impact:** May lead to data breaches and malware infection.
- **Prevention:** Refrain from utilizing untrusted devices, inform staff members of the dangers of accepting unsolicited offers, and put security procedures in place for managing external media.

Quid Pro Quo:

- **Definition**: Attackers, who frequently assume the identity of IT support or researchers, provide a reward in exchange for information or access.
- **Impact:** May result in sensitive data and systems being accessed without authorization.
- **Prevention:** Confirm the legality and identity of those extending help, set up processes for verifying

requests for IT support, and inform staff members on typical social engineering techniques.

Tailgating:

- **Definition:** Attackers follow authorized individuals to physically enter restricted locations.
- **Impact:** May cause unauthorized access to systems and sensitive locations.
- **Prevention:** Put in place stringent access controls, make use of biometric identification and security badges, and teach staff members how to spot and report suspicious activity.

Maintaining strong cybersecurity requires an understanding of and response to social engineering risks, which take advantage of human weaknesses rather than technical ones.

2.4 Insider Threats: Dangers Occurring Within Your Company

Employees, contractors, or business partners who abuse their access to do harm to the company are the source of insider threats.

Malicious Insiders:

- **Definition:** Those with authorized access who purposefully do harm by stealing information, breaking into systems, or disclosing private data.
- **Impact:** May result in severe financial loss, harm to one's reputation, and interruption of business operations.
- **Prevention:** Execute least privilege access controls, carry out extensive background checks, and keep an eye out for questionable conduct from users.

Employees with good intentions who inadvertently jeopardize security due to carelessness or ignorance are referred to as.

Accidental insiders:

- **Impact:** May lead to system vulnerabilities, compliance problems, and data breaches.
- **Prevention:** Adopt data loss prevention (DLP) programs, enforce strict password regulations, and conduct regular security training.

Third-Party Risks:

- **Definition:** Risks brought forth by vendors, contractors, or business associates who have access to the systems or data of the company.

- **Impact:** May result in financial loss, reputational damage, and data breaches.

- **Prevention:** Set stringent security guidelines for outside parties, carry out frequent security evaluations, and keep an eye on outsider access and activity.

A combination of technical controls, internal regulations, and staff training is needed to address insider threats in order to reduce risks and safeguard the company from internal dangers.

Creating successful cybersecurity tactics requires an awareness of and comprehension of frequent cyberattacks. People and organizations can better defend themselves against the constantly changing world of cyber dangers by being aware of the different kinds of risks, such as malware, phishing, social engineering, and insider threats.

CHAPTER 3

Fundamentals of Network Security: Safeguarding Your Digital Portals

Protecting users, systems, and data from cyber threats and unlawful access requires network security. This chapter explores fundamental network security techniques that serve as the cornerstone of a strong defense plan.

3.1 Firewalls: Constructing Barriers to Prevent Illegal Access

One of the main defenses against unwanted access to or from a private network is a firewall. They may be software- or hardware-based, or they may combine the two.

Definition and Function:

- In accordance with pre-established security regulations, firewalls keep an eye on all network traffic, both entering and leaving.

- They serve as a line of defense between unreliable external networks like the internet and reliable internal networks.

Firewall Types:

1. **Firewalls for Packet-Filtering:** Analyze packets at the network layer and filter according to protocols, ports, and source/destination IP addresses. Easy to use and effective, but might not be enough to counter complicated threats.

2. **Field-Proof Inspection Firewalls:** Keep tabs on the status of connections that are active and base your judgments on the traffic context. stronger than firewalls with packet filtering.

3. **Application-Layer Firewalls:** Examine data at the application layer, offering in-depth filtering options for particular protocols and apps.

4. **Next-Generation Firewalls (NGFWs):** Integrate cutting-edge features like threat intelligence, deep packet inspection, and intrusion prevention with conventional firewall capabilities.

Best Practices for Implementation:

- **Regular Updates:** Stay current with firewall firmware and software to guard against the most recent attacks.
- **Rule Configuration:** Make sure that all rules are well-defined and that only valid traffic is allowed while blocking potentially hazardous traffic.
- **Monitoring and Logging:** Keep track of all firewall activities and keep records in order to identify and examine unusual activity.

Setting up firewalls is essential for maintaining access control, creating a secure network perimeter, and defending against a variety of online threats.

3.2 Active Defenses for Intrusion Detection and Prevention Systems

In order to recognize and address possible attacks within a network, intrusion prevention systems (IPS) and intrusion detection systems (IDS) are essential.

Intrusion Detection Systems (IDS):

- **Function:** Notify administrators of potential dangers by keeping an eye on network traffic for unusual activities.

- **Types:**
    1. **Network-Based IDS (NIDS):** Keeps an eye on all network traffic for patterns of known attacks.
    2. **Host-Based IDS (HIDS)**: Keeps track of all system activities, including file changes and system calls.

Detection Techniques:

- **Signature-Based Detection:** Identifies known threats by using established patterns, or signatures. useful against established threats but may overlook fresh or undiscovered assaults.
- **Detection Based on Anomalies:** creates a baseline of typical activity and looks for variations from it. can spot novel or unidentified dangers, but it could also result in false positives.

Intrusion Prevention Systems (IPS):

- **Function:** Like intrusion detection systems (IDS), but with active real-time threat blocking or mitigation to stop attackers before they can cause damage.

- **Types:**
  - **Network-Based IPS (NIPS):** Located inside the network to obstruct erroneous data.
  - **Host-Based IPS (HIPS):** Set up on each machine to defend against nearby attacks.

Best Practices for Implementation:

- **Regular Updates:** Ensure that IDS/IPS signatures and rules are current in order to identify and address the most recent attacks.
- **Tuning and Configuration:** Adjust detection rules to minimize false positives while simultaneously recognizing real threats.
- **Integration with Other Security Tools:** Ascertain that firewalls and security information and event management (SIEM) systems, among other security measures, are seamlessly integrated with IDS/IPS.

By actively defending against network intrusions, deploying IDS and IPS can assist identify and stop unwanted activity that could jeopardize network security.

3.3 Segmenting the Network to Lower the Attack Surface

To improve security and manageability, a network can be segmented by breaking it up into smaller, more isolated parts.

Introduction and Advantages:
- **Protection:** Prevents malware and unwanted access by restricting it to certain areas.
- **Performance:** Reduces congestion and lessens the effect of local problems to improve network performance.
- **Compliance:** By separating sensitive data and systems, it is possible to comply with regulatory obligations.

Types of Segmentation:

- **Physical Segmentation:** Divides a network's segments into independent physical infrastructures. Extremely secure, however implementation can be costly and difficult.

- **Logical Segmentation:** Separates segments within the same physical network using technologies such as Virtual Local Area Networks, or VLANs. economical and adaptable.

Best Practices for Implementation:

- **Identify Critical Assets:** Ascertain whether data and systems require isolation for security reasons.

- **Establish Explicit Segmentation Policies:** Specify the reasons and methods for segment creation, making sure that they complement security objectives.

- **Implement Access Controls:** To regulate traffic across segments, use firewalls and ACLs (Access Control Lists).

- **Monitor and Maintain Segments:** To make sure segments stay safe and functional, periodically evaluate segmentation regulations and keep an eye on traffic.

By decreasing the attack surface, network segmentation helps to control and mitigate possible breaches by making it more difficult for cyber threats to travel laterally across a network.

3.4 Multi-factor authentication and strong passwords: The first line of defense

Multi-factor authentication (MFA) and strong passwords are essential elements of network security that operate as the first line of defense against illegal access.

Difficult Passwords:

Features:

- **Size:** Passwords must have a minimum of 12 characters.
- **Complexity:** Make use of a combination of special characters, numerals, and capital and lowercase letters.
- **Unpredictability:** Steer clear of utilizing

information that may be guessed, such as birthdays, frequent terms, or short word sequences.

Optimal Techniques:

- **Tools for Password Management:** Create and save secure, one-of-a-kind passwords for various accounts by using password managers.
- **Regular Updates:** Don't reuse passwords across accounts; instead, change them on a regular basis.
- **Education:** Inform users of the value of and procedures for creating strong passwords.

Multi-Factor Authentication (MFA):

- **Definition**: MFA goes beyond password security by requiring users to provide two or more verification factors in order to get access.

Types of Factors:

Passwords or PINs are examples of

1. **Item You Own:** Tangible items such as smart cards, security tokens, or cellphones. (Passwords or PINs.)
2. **Something You Are:** Biometric authentication by iris scans, fingerprints, or facial recognition.

The following are:

Best Practices for Implementation:

- **Universal Adoption:** Integrate MFA into all vital apps and systems.
- **User ease:** To promote wider adoption, select MFA techniques that strike a balance between security and user ease.
- **Regular evaluate:** To meet emerging security threats and technological advancements, periodically evaluate and update MFA policies.

Even in the event that passwords are compromised, the usage of MFA and strong passwords greatly enhances network security by making it more difficult for unauthorized users to obtain access.

To sum up, network security is crucial for shielding digital assets from various online dangers. Organizations can safeguard their digital doors and create a strong defense against prospective assaults by putting firewalls, IDS/IPS, network segmentation, and robust authentication methods into place.

CHAPTER 4

Safeguarding Your Digital Resources with Data Security

In the current digital era, data security is critical. It is crucial to protect your data from loss, theft, and illegal access, whether it is for personal or professional use. This chapter examines the fundamentals of data security, with thorough explanations of data management, encryption, backup and recovery strategies, and privacy settings.

4.1 Encryption: Digital Locks Protect Your Data

A basic method of data protection is encryption, which turns data into an unreadable format so that only people with the right decryption key may access it.

Definition and Significance:

- **Encryption:** The process of utilizing an encryption key and algorithm to transform plaintext into ciphertext.

- **Decryption:** The opposite procedure, which employs a decryption key to convert ciphertext back into legible plaintext.
- **Value:** Data is protected by encryption both in transit and at rest, guaranteeing confidentiality and integrity even in the event that data is intercepted or read without permission.

Types of Encryption:

- **Symmetric Encryption:** Encrypts and decrypts data using the same key. Although it is quicker, secure key management is necessary to make sure the key is secure.
    - **Models:** Data Encryption Standard (DES), Advanced Encryption Standard (AES).
- **Asymmetric Encryption:** Makes use of a public and private key pair. By separating the keys, the public key encrypts data and the private key decrypts it, increasing security.
    - RSA (Rivest-Shamir-Adleman) and ECC (Elliptic Curve Cryptography) are two examples.

Best Practices for Implementation:

- **Sturdy Algorithms:** To guarantee strong encryption, use industry-standard algorithms (such AES-256 and RSA-2048).

- **Key Management**: Put safe key management procedures into place, such as frequent key rotation and security against unwanted access.

- **Encryption at All Stages:** Protect sensitive information both in transit (data being sent across networks) and at rest (stored data).

A strong tool that secures your data digitally is encryption, which makes sure that only people with the right key can view and access private data.

4.2 Data Loss Prevention: Stopping Inadvertent or Malevolent Disclosures

The term "Data Loss Prevention" (DLP) refers to a set of techniques and instruments intended to stop sensitive data from being improperly shared, leaked, or destroyed.

Definition and Purpose:

- **DLP:** A collection of procedures and instruments for identifying and averting sensitive data breaches, exfiltration, and unintentional deletion.
- **Goal:** Preserve confidential data from unintentional disclosure or theft, maintaining data integrity and adhering to legal obligations.

DLP Components:

- **Identification:** Categorizing sensitive data according to established standards and guidelines.
- **Monitoring:** Constantly keeping an eye on the flow and consumption of data among endpoints, devices, and networks.
- **Protection:** enforcing regulations to stop illegal access, transfer, or erasure of private information.

Best Practices for Implementation:

- **Data Classification:** Determine and group data according to its significance and level of sensitivity (e.g., private, internal use only).
- **Policy Definition:** Clearly define DLP policies and put them into effect, outlining how data should be managed and safeguarded.

- **User Education:** Educate staff members on DLP guidelines, stressing the value of data security and the dangers of data loss.
- **Regular Audits:** To guarantee adherence to DLP policies and pinpoint areas in need of development, conduct audits and evaluations on a regular basis.

Organizations can greatly lower the risk of data breaches and leaks by putting DLP protections in place, safeguarding sensitive data from both unintentional and intentional threats.

4.3 Data Recovery and Backup: Ready for the Worst

A thorough data security plan must include data backup and recovery to guarantee that information can be recovered in the case of loss, corruption, or disaster.

Concept and Significance:

- **Data backup:** The act of making duplicate copies of data in order to guard against damage, loss, or corruption.
- **Data Recovery:** the process of using backups to

restore lost, corrupted, or damaged data.

- **Value:** Frequent backups minimize downtime and data loss in the event of an incident by ensuring that data can be restored promptly and effectively.

Data Backup Types:

- **Full Backup:** An exact duplicate of all data. Although thorough, it requires a lot of time and resources.

- **Step-by-Step Backup:** only copies the information that has changed since the previous backup. quicker and more effective, but a full restoration necessitates several backups.

- **Redundant Backup:** Data copies have evolved since the last complete backup. strikes a balance between the effectiveness of incremental backups and the thoroughness of complete backups.

Best Practices for Implementation:

- **Regular Backups:** Arrange regular backups to guarantee that the most recent data is safeguarded.

- **Offsite Storage:** To guard against natural disasters like fires and floods, store backups in a safe offsite

location.

- **Testing and Verification:** Make sure data can be successfully restored by regularly testing backups.

- **Automated Solutions:** To lower the possibility of human error and guarantee consistency, use automated backup solutions.

Organizations may guarantee business continuity and data integrity even in the face of unforeseen occurrences by arming themselves with strong data backup and recovery procedures.

4.4 Data management and privacy settings: Taking charge of your information

By giving people and organizations more control over the collection, use, and sharing of personal data, privacy settings and data management techniques improve data security and adhere to privacy laws.

Privacy Settings:

- **Definition:** User-configurable settings that regulate how websites, apps, and services gather, use, and

share user data.

- **Value:** Sufficient privacy configurations aid in preventing unwanted access to and exploitation of sensitive data.

Privacy Settings' Principal Domains:

- **Personal Data:** Manage who has access to and can share personal data (such as name, address, and contact details).
- **Location Data:** Control the rights granted to services and applications that track or make use of location data.
- **Cookies and Tracking:** Modify cookie and tracking technology settings to restrict data gathering and customized advertising.

The process of efficiently and securely arranging, storing, and managing data is known as:

Data Management:

- **Value:** Accuracy, integrity, and security of data are ensured by effective data management, enabling both regulatory compliance and company operations.

Best Practices for Data Management:

- **Data Minimization:** To lower the risk of exposure, collect and keep just the data required for particular reasons.

- **Access restrictions:** Put role-based access restrictions in place to make sure that only people with permission can access sensitive information.

- **Data Lifecycle Management:** To manage data throughout its lifecycle, define and implement policies for data archiving, disposal, and retention.

- **Regular Audits:** Review data management procedures and make sure rules and regulations are being followed by conducting audits on a regular basis.

Through the management of privacy settings and the adoption of efficient data management procedures, people and institutions can safeguard their data, improve data security, and adhere to privacy laws.

Data security is crucial for shielding digital assets from all types of attacks. Organizations can create a strong defense

strategy that protects their data, upholds compliance, and guarantees business continuity by utilizing encryption, data loss prevention, data backup and recovery, privacy settings, and data management.

CHAPTER 5

Data Security in the Cloud: Protecting Your Information

As more and more businesses move their data and apps to the cloud, it's critical to comprehend cloud security and put strong safeguards in place. Here explores the fundamentals of cloud security, such as comprehending cloud security models, protecting cloud storage, assessing cloud application security vendor practices, and managing data sovereignty and compliance.

5.1 Comprehending Shared Responsibility in Cloud Security Models

Security in cloud computing is a shared duty between the client and the cloud service provider (CSP). Comprehending this concept is essential to guaranteeing all-encompassing cloud security.

Definition and Significance:

- **Model of Shared Responsibilities:** a structure that outlines the customer's and CSP's respective security obligations. Generally speaking, the client is in charge of protecting their data and apps in the cloud, while the CSP is in charge of protecting the cloud infrastructure.

- **Value:** By clearly defining roles, it is ensured that everyone knows their part in keeping cloud security up to date and preventing security lapses.

Shared Responsibility Model Components:

CSP Responsibilities:

- **Infrastructure Security:** Taking care of data centers' and hardware's physical and network security.

- **Platform Security:** Offering safe operating systems and virtualization environments.

- **Compliance:** Upholding adherence to rules and industry norms.

Asset Responsibilities for Customers:

- **Encrypting data** while it's in transit and at rest is data security.
- **Application Security:** Putting vulnerability management and secure coding techniques into effect.
- **Identity and Access Management:** Regulating permissions and user access.

Best Practices for Implementation:

- **Knowing Your Boundaries:** Clearly identify and comprehend the limits of the CSP's and the customer's responsibilities.
- **Regular Communication:** Stay up to date on security updates and responsibilities by keeping lines of communication open with the CSP.
- **Comprehensive Policies:** Create thorough security policies that cover the duties of both customers and CSPs.

Organizations can work together with their cloud service providers (CSPs) to guarantee strong cloud security by comprehending and putting the shared responsibility concept into practice.

stored on the cloud. Organizations may secure their digital assets and guarantee the integrity and confidentiality of their data in the cloud by comprehending cloud security models, adopting data sovereignty and compliance measures, reviewing vendor practices for cloud application security, and safeguarding cloud storage

CHAPTER 6

Mobile Security: Safeguarding Your Portable Electronics

Ensuring the security of mobile devices is crucial in an era where they play a vital role in everyday life and commercial operations. Essential elements of mobile security are covered in this chapter, such as protecting cell phones, realizing the dangers of public Wi-Fi, identifying mobile malware threats, and creating plans for data backup and recovery in case of lost or stolen devices.

6.1 Protecting Your Smartphone: Updates, Permissions, and Passwords

Smartphones are veritable gold mines of sensitive and private data. To secure data from unwanted access, various levels of protection must be in place.

Authentication and Passwords:

- **Strong Passwords:** For device access, use passphrases or difficult, one-of-a-kind passwords. Avert using passwords that are simple to figure out, like "123456" or "password."

- **Biometric Authentication:** To provide an extra degree of protection, enable biometric features like fingerprint or facial recognition.

- **Double-Factor Verification (2FA):** To provide an additional layer of protection, use 2FA for important apps and services.

Software Updates on a Regular Basis:

- **Importance:** Vulnerability fixes are included in software upgrades often. It's essential to update the apps and operating system on your smartphone to guard against emerging risks.

- **Updates Automatically:** To guarantee that you get the most recent security patches as soon as they are issued, turn on automatic updates.

App Permissions:

- **Review Permissions:** Make sure that apps are only able to access the information and features that are required by regularly reviewing and managing app permissions.

- **Least Privilege concept:** Implement this concept by giving programs the minimal amount of permissions necessary for them to operate.

Users can greatly improve the security of their cellphones by putting these precautions in place, shielding confidential information from potential breaches and illegal access.

6.2 Risks Associated with Public Wi-Fi: Safe Connections While Traveling

Despite their convenience, public Wi-Fi networks present serious security threats. Mobile security requires knowing these hazards and implementing safe habits when utilizing public Wi-Fi.

Public Wi-Fi Risks:

Man-in-the-Middle Attacks:

- These attacks allow third parties to eavesdrop on and control data that is sent back and forth between your device and the Wi-Fi network.

- **Unsecured Networks:** A lot of open Wi-Fi networks don't have encryption, which makes it simpler for hackers to intercept your data.
- **Rogue Hotspots:** Cybercriminals might create fictitious Wi-Fi networks in order to obtain private data from gullible individuals.

Safeguarding Your Link:

- **Virtual Private Network (VPN)**: Encrypt your internet traffic with a VPN to keep your information safe from eavesdropping.
- **Avoid Sensitive Transactions:** Steer clear of sensitive account access and avoid using public Wi-Fi for financial transactions.
- **HTTPS:** Make sure that websites that communicate securely use HTTPS. In the address bar of the browser, look for the padlock icon.

Wi-Fi Settings:

- **Turn Off Auto-Connect:** Turn off auto-connect to stop your device from connecting to unsafe networks on its own.

- **Nevermind Networks:** To prevent connecting automatically to possibly compromised networks, regularly remove networks from your list of saved networks.

Users can safeguard their data and privacy when on the go by being aware of the hazards connected with public Wi-Fi and implementing secure habits.

6.3 Mobile Malware Threats: Recognizing the Dangers Apps Pose

Malware, which is frequently delivered through malicious programs, is increasingly aimed towards mobile devices. Mobile security depends on identifying these threats and putting preventative measures in place.

Types of Mobile Malware:

Mobile Malware Types:
Adware: Unwanted advertisements are displayed on your device, frequently causing it to lag and use more data.
Spyware: surreptitiously gathers and monitors personal

data without the user's permission.

Trojan: poses as trustworthy software but, once installed, does nasty things.

Ransomware: encrypts the data on the device and requests payment to unlock it.

Preventing Mobile Malware Infections:

- **Download from Reliable Sources**: Make sure you only download apps from reliable stores like the Apple App Store or Google Play Store.

- **App Reviews and Ratings:** Verify the legitimacy and trustworthiness of app reviews and ratings before downloading.

- **Permissions Scrutiny:** Apps that ask for a lot of permissions that don't seem to be necessary for their functionality should be avoided.

- **Mobile Security Software:** Set up a dependable program that can identify and stop malware threats on your mobile device.

Anti-Malware Scans:

- **Regular Scans and Update**s: Use mobile security software to conduct routine scans in order to identify and eliminate possible threats.

- **Remember to Update Apps:** Make sure all applications are updated on a regular basis to fix security holes that malware might exploit.

Through knowledge of the different kinds of mobile malware and the implementation of preventive measures, users may protect their devices and data against harmful interference.

6.4 Data Backup and Recovery Techniques for Missing or Stolen Devices

A mobile device that is lost or stolen may result in serious data loss and security breaches. To reduce these risks, data backup and recovery techniques must be put into place.

Data Backup:

- Cloud Backups: Ensure that you have a regular backup of your device's data to a safe cloud service in case it becomes lost or stolen.
- **Relative Positions:** For an extra degree of security, create regular local backups to a computer or

external storage device.

Device Recovery Features:

- **Find My Device:** Turn on device tracking functions to remotely find, lock, or wipe a lost device. Examples of these functions include "Find My iPhone" and "Find My Device" (Android).

- **Remote Wipe:** To avoid unwanted access to private data, use the remote wipe feature to remove data from a lost or stolen device.

Protective Steps for Misplaced Devices:

- **Lock Screen Security:** Verify that your device has a robust lock screen security mechanism (password, PIN, or biometrics) to thwart unwanted access.

- **Notify the Authorities:** To ban the device and stop misuse, report stolen devices to your cell service provider and local authorities.

Users can lessen the effects of lost or stolen devices by putting strong data backup and recovery procedures in place, guaranteeing that their data is safe and recoverable.

Mobile security is crucial for safeguarding private and sensitive data when on the road. Users may protect their mobile devices and preserve their digital privacy and security by safeguarding cell phones, comprehending the dangers of using public Wi-Fi, identifying mobile malware threats, and creating efficient data backup and recovery plans.

CHAPTER 7

Protecting Connected Devices with the Internet of Things (IoT) Security

The Internet of Things (IoT), which offers previously unheard-of efficiency and ease, has completely changed the way we engage with technology. On the other hand, as linked devices proliferate, so does the attack surface for cyber attacks. This chapter examines the emergence of the Internet of Things (IoT), the security issues raised by smart home gadgets, the weaknesses in connected infrastructure, and the prospects for IoT security through standards and cooperative efforts.

7.1 Internet of Things Growth: Increasing the Attack Surface

An extensive network of interconnected devices that exchange data and communicate online is referred to as the Internet of Things. IoT devices have become essential to contemporary living and commercial operations, ranging from smart household appliances to industrial control systems. But increased connectedness also means more security risks.

Demand for IoT Devices:

- **Proliferation:** With billions of devices currently online, the number of IoT devices has increased dramatically. These consist of industrial sensors, wearable health monitors, and smart thermostats.
- **Diversity:** The functionality and complexity of IoT devices range greatly, from basic sensors to sophisticated automation systems.

Expanded Area of Attack:

- **Points of Vulnerability for Ingress:** Every Internet of Things device is a possible point of entry for attackers. A single device's inadequate security can put the network as a whole at risk.
- **Networks of Systems:** IoT devices are interconnected, therefore an assault on one might potentially cause more harm than intended by cascading effects on other devices.

Difficulties with IoT Security:

- **Resource Limitations:** A lot of IoT devices have low processing and memory capacities, which makes it difficult to put strong security measures in place.

- **Inadequate Harmonization:** Inconsistent security standards and practices result from the variety of IoT devices and manufacturers.

The attack surface has grown dramatically as a result of the growth of IoT, calling for a thorough strategy to secure connected devices and reduce possible dangers.

7.2 Safeguarding Smart Home Appliances: Recognizing Deficiencies

Convenience and automation are provided by smart home appliances, but they also provide security flaws that hackers might take advantage of. Comprehending these susceptibilities is crucial for safeguarding intelligent living spaces.

Common Vulnerabilities:

- **Weak Passwords:** A lot of smart home appliances use default passwords that are simple to figure out or that users haven't changed.

- **Unpatched Software:** Updates to firmware and software are essential for fixing security flaws, but a lot of devices are still unpatched because of user error or a lack of manufacturer support.

- **Insecure Communication:** Certain devices employ communication protocols that are not encrypted, leaving data vulnerable to manipulation and interception.

Securing Smart Home Devices:

- **Change Default Passwords:** As soon as possible, replace each device's default password with a strong, one-of-a-kind password.

- **Regular Updates:** To guarantee that known vulnerabilities are patched, keep the software and firmware on your devices up to date.

- **Network Segmentation:** To isolate IoT devices from vital systems and lessen the possible impact of a breach, create distinct network segments for them.

- **Secure Communication:** To safeguard data transmission, use devices that enable encrypted communication protocols.

Users can dramatically increase the security of their networked settings by being aware of and taking action against the vulnerabilities present in smart home devices.

7.3 Connected Infrastructure Weaknesses: Protecting Critical Systems

IoT technologies are becoming more and more important to connected infrastructure, which includes crucial utilities and industrial control systems. It is essential to secure these systems to avoid potentially disastrous disruptions.

Connected Infrastructure Vulnerabilities:
- **Legacy Systems:** A lot of vital infrastructure systems were created before contemporary cybersecurity threats emerged, so they don't have the necessary security measures in place.
- **Remote Access:** Although useful, remote access features can be exploited by attackers if inadequately

secured.

- **Relatedness:** Because infrastructure systems are interconnected, a targeted attack on one component can have a significant impact on other systems.

Securing Critical Systems:

- **Risk Assessment:** Identify vulnerabilities and rank security measures according to detailed risk evaluations.
- **Access restrictions:** To stop unwanted access to vital systems, enforce stringent access restrictions and monitoring.
- **Regular Audits:** To find and fix vulnerabilities, conduct regular penetration tests and security audits.
- **Incident Response:** Create thorough incident response plans and put them into action right away to address and minimize security breaches.

An all-encompassing, proactive strategy that includes risk assessments, access controls, frequent audits, and incident response planning is needed to secure connected infrastructure.

7.4 Standards and Cooperation in the Future of IoT Security

Stakeholder cooperation and the creation of thorough standards to guarantee the security of linked devices are essential to the future of IoT security.

Collaborative Efforts:

- **Industrial Collaboration:** To create and execute best practices for IoT security, manufacturers, cybersecurity companies, and standards bodies must collaborate.
- **Government Involvement:** By passing laws and offering guidelines to improve IoT security, governments can play a significant role.
- **Public Awareness:** Building a user base that is security-conscious requires educating the public about IoT security threats and best practices.

Standards Development:

- **Security Frameworks:** Creating security frameworks and standards can offer a standardized method of safeguarding IoT devices across various producers and sectors.

- **Certification Programs:** Prior to a product's release onto the market, certification programs for Internet of Things devices can assist guarantee that it complies with security standards.
- **Ongoing Studies:** To remain ahead of new threats and create cutting-edge security solutions, research and development must continue.

The future of IoT security may be reinforced by encouraging cooperation and creating thorough standards, guaranteeing that linked devices are safe and resistant to changing threats.

In light of the increasing number of IoT devices and their growing attack surface, it is imperative to secure them. We can improve IoT security and secure our connected world by comprehending vulnerabilities, safeguarding smart home gadgets, safeguarding important infrastructure, and encouraging cooperative efforts and standards.

CHAPTER 8

Understanding Data Collection Practices in the Digital Age of Privacy

Maintaining privacy in the digital age requires a grasp of how data is gathered, utilized, and safeguarded. This chapter explores the mechanics behind social media privacy management, online monitoring, shielding against targeted advertising, and complying with data privacy laws such as CCPA and GDPR.

8.1 Internet Tracking and Cookies: How Information About You Is Gathered

In the digital era, cookies and online monitoring are commonplace and have a big impact on user profiling and data gathering.

Cookies:

Cookie definition:

- **Cookies:** are little text files that websites you visit keep on your device. This includes browsing history, preferences, and login credentials. They are used to save information about your visit.

Types of Cookies:

1. **Session Cookies:** One-time cookies that are removed from your computer when you close your browser.
2. **Persistent Cookies**: Last for a predetermined amount of time or until you consciously remove them from your device.
3. **First-Party Cookies:** Those placed by the website you are currently viewing.
4. **Third-Party Cookies:** Ads and tracking cookies placed by domains other than the one you are currently on.

Virtual Tracking:

- **Methods of Tracking:** In addition to cookies, user

activity across websites is monitored through the use of web beacons, pixels, and fingerprinting.

- **Information Got:** contains information about devices, IP addresses, search queries, and browsing histories. With this information, comprehensive profiles of users' internet activity can be created.

Concerns Regarding Privacy:

- **User Profiling:** Detailed user profiles are generated, which are useful for behavioral analysis and targeted advertising.
- **Exchange of Data:** Data security and privacy issues are brought up by the frequent sharing of collected data with analytics firms and outside advertisers.

Users may manage their data more efficiently and make educated decisions about their online privacy by being aware of the workings of cookies and tracking.

8.2 Social Media Privacy: Taking Control of Your Online Identity

Users must carefully control their online appearance and

privacy settings on social media platforms because these sites gather enormous amounts of personal data about them.

Data Collection by Social Media:

Social media is used to collect data.

- **The types of data collected are as follows**: activity data (likes, shares, posts), behavioral data (interactions, engagement), and personal information (name, age, location).
- **Access from a Third Party**: Users' data is frequently shared by social media platforms with advertisers and third-party apps.

Managing Privacy Settings:

To manage what information is shared and with whom, regularly check and update privacy settings (see Managing Privacy Settings:).

- **Reviewing Permissions:** Regularly review and adjust privacy settings to control what information is shared and with whom.

-
- **Reducing Personal Information:** Try to share as little personal information as possible on social media platforms.
- **Two-Factor Authentication:** Allow two-factor verification to improve account security.

Preserving Your Online Image:

- **Conscientious Disclosure:** Exercise caution while disclosing information online, taking into account the possible long-term consequences.
- **Regular Audits:** Regularly review your social media profiles to eliminate personal information that is no longer relevant or needless.

Users may keep control over their digital footprint and safeguard their personal information by actively monitoring their privacy settings and being aware of what they post online.

8.3 Personalized Advertising: Disabling It and Safeguarding Your Preferences

Concerns over data collection and use privacy are brought up by targeted advertising, which uses personal information to offer customized ads.

Targeted Advertising Mechanisms:

- **Data Sources:** Search searches, browsing and purchase histories, and social media activity are the sources of data used in targeted advertising.
- **Ad Networks:** Businesses like Google and Facebook analyze data and present tailored advertisements using complex algorithms.

Protective Issues:

- **Overreaching**: Since targeted advertisements frequently expose the extent of firms' knowledge about personal preferences and activities, they might be perceived as intrusive.
- **Safeguarding Data:** Targeted advertising necessitates considerable data collecting, which raises the possibility of data breaches and misuse.

Choosing Not to Participate in Targeted Advertising:

- **Ad Settings:** Utilize ad settings on websites such as Google and Facebook to restrict the usage of personal information for advertising.

- **Browser Extensions:** To improve privacy, install browser extensions that prevent advertisements and trackers.

- **Do Not Track:** Turn on web browsers' "Do Not Track" option to express a preference not to be tracked.

Users can lessen the impact of targeted advertising and better secure their personal data by utilizing privacy-enhancing technologies and opting out of certain offers.

8.4 Regulations Concerning Data Privacy: GDPR, CCPA, and Other

The General Data Protection Regulation (GDPR) and the California Consumer Privacy Act (CCPA) are two examples of data privacy laws that seek to safeguard individuals' personal information while granting them more choice over how it is used.

The General Data Protection Regulation (GDPR):

- **The Application:** This regulation covers all companies, regardless of location, that process the personal data of residents of the European Union.

The following are the main provisions:

- **Data Subject Rights:** These include the ability to access, correct, delete, and limit the use of personal data.
- **Consent:** Requires explicit, affirmative consent before processing data.
- **Data Protection Officers:** Data Protection Officers (DPOs) are required to be appointed by organizations in order to supervise compliance.
- **Breach Notification:** Required notification of data breaches to authorities within a 72-hour period.

California Consumer Privacy Act (CCPA):

- The **Scope:** California Consumer Privacy Act (CCPA) applies to companies that meet specific requirements and gather personal information from

California consumers.

Essential Requirements:

- **Consumer Rights:** Includes the right to request the deletion of personal information, the right to know what personal information is collected, and the right to refuse to have your personal information sold.
- **Transparency:** Companies are required to reveal how they gather and share personal information.
- **Penalties**: Imposes fines for noncompliance and offers a private right of action in the event of private data breaches.

Global Effect and Additional Regulations:

- **CCPA and GDPR Influence**: These laws have impacted legislation in other areas and established a standard for data privacy around the globe.
- **Other Regulations:** Nations with developed or pending data privacy legislation include Australia, Brazil, Canada, and Australia.

It is imperative for firms to comprehend and adhere to data privacy standards in order to safeguard personal information and foster consumer trust.

Managing privacy in the digital age necessitates knowledge of data gathering methods, efficient social media privacy management, techniques to avoid targeted advertising, and compliance with data privacy laws. People and businesses may guarantee a more secure digital experience and better protect their personal information by being proactive and knowledgeable.

CHAPTER 9

Encouraging Users to Develop a Cybersecurity Culture

Protecting sensitive data and systems in the digital age requires organizations to establish a cybersecurity culture. This chapter examines the essential elements of creating such a culture, such as training staff, putting defenses to the test, keeping systems up to date, and making incident response plans.

9.1 Cybersecurity Awareness Education for Individuals and Staff

An essential component of creating a strong cybersecurity culture is cybersecurity awareness training. It entails teaching staff members and people in general about possible security risks and recommended security procedures.

Value of Training:

- **Identifying Threats:** Employees that have received training are better able to identify malware, phishing scams, and other online dangers.

- **Behavioral Change:** Employees are more likely to adopt secure practices if they recognize the significance of cybersecurity.

- **Risk Reduction:** Knowledgeable staff members are less likely to become targets of cyberattacks, which lowers the organization's total risk.

Elements of Successful Training:

- **Regular Sessions:** Hold training sessions on a regular basis to maintain current cybersecurity knowledge.

- **Interactive Learning:** To keep people interested, use interactive techniques including games, role-playing, and practical activities.

- **Tailored Content:** Adapt training materials to the unique requirements and weaknesses of the company.

Primary Subjects to Address:

- **Social Engineering and Phishing:** Inform on how to spot and steer clear of social engineering and phishing schemes.

- **Password Security:** Stress the value of using multi-factor authentication and creating strong passwords.

- **Safe Browsing Practices:** Explain the dangers of downloading untrusted content and encourage safe browsing practices.

By allocating resources for thorough cybersecurity awareness training, companies can enable their staff to serve as the first line of defense against online attacks.

9.2 Phishing Simulations: Examining Users' Reactions to Trickery

Phishing simulators are a proactive way to evaluate and fortify a company's defenses against deceptive online threats.

Intention behind Phishing Simulations:

- **Practical Testing:** Model actual phishing attacks to assess workers' reactions.

- **Identify Weaknesses:** Find out where staff members could be at risk from phishing scams.

- **Reinforce instruction:** Give students hands-on practice spotting phishing emails to reinforce cybersecurity instruction.

Creating Powerful Simulations:

- **Creating Realistic Scenarios:** Craft phishing emails that, both in appearance and content, resemble actual attacks.

- **Different Difficulty Levels:** Vary the degree of difficulty to assess staff members' comprehension of various phishing attempt kinds.

- **Immediate Feedback:** Following a simulation, give staff members prompt feedback to help them learn from their mistakes and make improvements.

Phishing Simulation Benefits:

- **Increased Awareness:** Consistent simulations raise staff members' awareness of phishing techniques.

- **Reduced Risk:** Organizations can lower the likelihood that successful phishing attacks will occur by detecting and fixing holes.
- **Improved Response:** Workers get better at seeing and reporting phishing attempts, which improves security in general.

As part of the cybersecurity plan, phishing simulations are used to assist strengthen defenses against one of the most prevalent types of cyberattacks.

9.3 Patch Management's Significance: Keeping Systems Updated

Patch management is an essential procedure that includes updating systems and software on a regular basis to guard against vulnerabilities.

Why Patch Management Is Important:
- **Vulnerability Mitigation**: Patches fix security flaws that hackers might use against you.
- **System Stability:** Frequent upgrades minimize the chance of crashes and downtime by ensuring that

systems operate smoothly and efficiently.

- **Accordance:** Organizations must keep their software up to date in order to protect sensitive data, as mandated by numerous legislation and standards.

Effective Patch Management Strategies:

- **Automated Updates:** Manage and install fixes quickly with the help of automated tools.
- **Regular Scanning:** Check systems on a regular basis for vulnerabilities and missing fixes.
- **Prioritization:** Set patch priorities according to the criticality of the impacted systems and the seriousness of the vulnerabilities they address.

Difficulties with Patch Management:

- **Compatibility Problems:** Making sure that updates don't interfere with already-installed programs or systems.
- **Resource Constraints:** Assigning enough staff and resources to properly manage and apply patches.
- **User Resistance**: Getting over users' reluctance to update their systems because they think it will cause them inconvenience.

Organizations may guarantee the continuous security and reliability of their systems and drastically lower their susceptibility to cyber threats by putting in place a strong patch management procedure.

9.4 Event Response Strategy: Lessening the Effects of Attacks

To effectively manage and reduce the consequences of cyberattacks, a company must have an incident response plan in place.

The Incident Response Planning Goal:

- **Quick Recovery:** Facilitate the prompt detection and containment of security issues in order to reduce damage.
- **Structured Response:** Manage incidents in a clear, organized manner to cut down on confusion and downtime.
- **Regulatory Compliance:** Make sure that incident reporting and response procedures adhere to all applicable laws and regulations.

The following are the essential elements of an incident response plan:

- **Incident Identification:** Set up procedures for spotting and recognizing possible security incidents.
- **Roles and duties:** Clearly define the incident response team's roles and duties to ensure accountability.
- **Communication Plan:** Create a communication strategy for customers, regulatory agencies, and other internal and external stakeholders.

Incident Response Steps:
- **Preparation:** Create and update the incident response plan, carry out frequent drills and training sessions.
- **Detection and Analysis:** Keep an eye out for any indications of an issue and assess the extent and type of the problem by monitoring systems.
- **Containment and Eradication:** To stop additional harm, contain the occurrence and get rid of the underlying cause.

- Restore the impacted systems and data, and confirm that vulnerabilities have been fixed.
- **Post-Incident Review**: To find lessons learned and enhance subsequent responses, thoroughly examine the incident and the response activities.

Incident Response Planning Benefits:

- **Minimized Impact:** A successful incident response can drastically lower the cost and impact of a cyberattack.
- **Enhanced Preparedness:** The organization's readiness for upcoming incidents is guaranteed by routinely testing and upgrading the incident response plan.
- **Increased Confidence:** Stakeholders, consumers, and staff all feel more confident when they know a plan is in place.

To mitigate the effects of cyberattacks and respond to them quickly, it is imperative for any firm to invest in a thorough incident response plan.

Fostering a cybersecurity culture inside a company entails

keeping systems updated through patch management, testing defenses using phishing simulations, educating staff members through awareness training, and being ready for emergencies with a well-thought-out reaction plan. Through user empowerment and proactive security culture development, businesses may strengthen their defenses against the dynamic threat landscape.

CHAPTER 10

Cybersecurity and Privacy in the Future: Emerging Risks and Solutions

The cybersecurity and privacy landscape is always changing as the digital age advances, bringing with it both new opportunities and difficulties. This chapter examines new risks and creative fixes that will influence privacy and cybersecurity in the future.

10.1 Machine learning and artificial intelligence: security implications

Cybersecurity is one of the many industries that artificial intelligence (AI) and machine learning (ML) are creating waves in. These technologies come with new security considerations in addition to their many benefits.

Intelligence and Machine Learning in Cybersecurity:

- **Introduced Threat Identification:** AI and ML are

capable of sifting through enormous volumes of data to find trends and abnormalities that could point to a security breach. These innovations improve the capacity to anticipate and stop attacks before they happen.

- **Automated Responses:** AI-powered solutions have the ability to automate security issue responses, speeding up reaction times and minimizing damage.
- **Behavioral Analysis:** Machine learning algorithms are able to track user behavior and identify anomalous activity that could indicate a breach.

AI and ML Security Challenges:

- **Adversarial Attacks:** Cybercriminals can manipulate AI and ML models by feeding them false information, leading them to make erroneous choices.
- **Privacy Concerns for Data:** There are serious privacy concerns because AI and ML models demand enormous volumes of data to train. It is vital to guarantee data protection when utilizing these technologies.
- **Algorithmic Bias:** When it comes to automated

decision-making processes, biases in AI algorithms might result in unfair or discriminatory behaviors.

Future directions include:

- **Robust AI Models:** Creating ML and AI models that are resistant to biases and adversarial attacks.
- **Privacy-Preserving Techniques**: Using strategies like differential privacy to safeguard personal information while utilizing AI and ML capabilities.
- **Ethical AI Practices:** Creating moral norms and rules to guarantee the ethical and just application of AI technologies.

In the future of cybersecurity, artificial intelligence (AI) and machine learning (ML) will be crucial tools for threat identification and response, but their security consequences must be carefully considered.

10.2 Ransomware-as-a-Service (RaaS): The Emergence

A growing threat that has changed the ransomware environment and made it simpler for cybercriminals to conduct assaults is called ransomware-as-a-service, or

RaaS.

Comprehending RaaS:

- **Enterprise Model:** Ransomware creators use the RaaS business model to rent their virus to affiliates. They get a portion of the ransom money in exchange.

- **Accessibility:** RaaS makes it easier for hackers to start their operations, enabling even individuals with little technological expertise to carry out ransomware assaults.

- **Adjustment:** Because RaaS platforms provide modifiable ransomware, affiliates can focus their attacks on certain targets.

Impact of RaaS:

The impact of ransomware assaults has increased due to the accessibility of malware, impacting enterprises across many sectors and sizes.

- **Increased Demands for Ransom:** The financial burden on victims has increased due to hackers' increased willingness to demand greater ransoms as a result of RaaS's popularity.

- **Wider Target variety:** RaaS makes it possible to attack a wider variety of targets, such as crucial infrastructure, small and medium-sized enterprises, and healthcare providers.

Limiting RaaS Risks:

- **Trainee Education:** Educating staff members on phishing and ransomware techniques to lower the probability of successful attacks.
- **frequent Backups:** Making sure data backups are stored safely and apart from the primary network on a frequent basis.
- **Advanced Security methods:** Using intrusion prevention systems (IPS) and endpoint detection and response (EDR) as examples of advanced security methods to identify and stop ransomware activity.

A multifaceted strategy combining staff education, stringent security procedures, and cutting-edge technical solutions is needed to counter the RaaS threat.

10.3 Quantum Computing: Possible Dangers and Benefits

With the potential to completely transform a number of industries, including cybersecurity, quantum computing provides a substantial advancement in processing capacity.

Quantum Computing Fundamentals:

- **Quantum Bits (Qubits):** With the ability to represent many states concurrently, qubits allow for exponentially quicker computations than classical bits.
- **Quantum Algorithms:** Compared to classical algorithms, algorithms like Shor's algorithm can solve complex problems far more quickly.

Cryptographic Vulnerabilities:

Security Threats:

- Common cryptographic algorithms like RSA and ECC, which depend on the difficulty of factoring big numbers, may be broken by quantum computers.
- **Risks to Data Protection:** Long-term data

protection threats arise from the possibility that encrypted data that is safe now could one day be susceptible to decoding by quantum computers.

Applications and Solutions:

- **Quantum-Resistant Cryptography:** Creating and implementing cryptographic techniques, including lattice-based cryptography, that are immune to quantum attacks.

- **Quantum Key Distribution (QKD):** This technique creates secure communication channels that are theoretically impervious to eavesdropping by applying concepts from quantum mechanics.

Cybersecurity faces both opportunities and challenges from quantum computing. Shifting to quantum-resistant cryptographic solutions and investigating novel security technologies are necessary steps towards preparing for the arrival of quantum computing.

10.4 Innovation and Cooperation to Build a Resilient Future

The future of privacy and cybersecurity depends on cooperation and innovation. Through collaboration and use of novel technologies, we can construct a robust digital future.

Collaborative Efforts:

- **Information Sharing:** Promoting information exchange between governments, businesses, and organizations in order to enhance threat intelligence and response capacities.

- **Public-Private Partnerships:** Promoting collaborations between the public and private sectors in order to jointly solve cybersecurity issues and create all-encompassing solutions.

- **International Cooperation:** Encouraging collaboration between nations to combat cyberthreats that cut across national boundaries and guaranteeing a common approach to cybersecurity practices and policies.

Innovative Solutions:

- **Blockchain Technology:** Using the decentralized and tamper-proof features of blockchain technology to improve security across a range of applications, such as identity verification and supply chain management.

- **Zero Trust Architecture**: Using a zero trust security paradigm that constantly confirms the identity and integrity of devices and users while assuming there is no implicit trust within the network.

- **Artificial Intelligence Advancements:** We're still working to improve threat detection, automate responses, and forecast new cyberthreats by developing AI and ML technologies.

Creating a Resilient Workforce:

- **Investing in Cybersecurity Education:** To develop a workforce with the necessary skills to handle upcoming problems, funds should be allocated to cybersecurity education and training.

- **Diversity and Inclusion:** Fostering a diverse and inclusive environment in the cybersecurity industry to bring a range of viewpoints and creative solutions to challenging issues.

- **Continuous Learning:** Promoting a professional growth and learning culture in order to stay up to date with the rapidly changing landscape of cyber risks and technologies.

Collaboration, creativity, and constant improvement are key components of building a resilient future that can better address new privacy and cybersecurity issues.

The dynamic threat landscape and the quick pace of technological breakthroughs will continue to influence cybersecurity and privacy. We can make the digital world safer and more secure by comprehending and addressing the consequences of AI and ML, preventing the spread of ransomware-as-a-service, being ready for the effects of quantum computing, and encouraging creative and cooperative solutions. This book offers a thorough introduction to cybersecurity and privacy along with doable strategies for safeguarding your information in a constantly changing digital environment. We can make everyone's online experience safer and more secure by remaining informed and using best practices.

ABOUT THE AUTHOR

 Author and thought leader in the IT field Taylor Royce is well known. He has a two-decade career and is an expert at tech trend analysis and forecasting, which enables a wide audience to understand complicated concepts.

Royce's considerable involvement in the IT industry stemmed from his passion with technology, which he developed during his computer science studies. He has extensive knowledge of the industry because of his experience in both software development and strategic consulting.

Known for his research and lucidity, he has written multiple best-selling books and contributed to esteemed tech periodicals. Translations of Royce's books throughout the world demonstrate his impact.

Royce is a well-known authority on emerging technologies and their effects on society, frequently requested as a speaker at international conferences and as a guest on tech podcasts. He promotes the development of ethical technology, emphasizing problems like data privacy and the digital divide.

In addition, with a focus on sustainable industry growth, Royce mentors upcoming tech experts and supports IT education projects. Taylor Royce is well known for his ability to combine analytical thinking with technical know-how. He sees a time when technology will ethically benefit humanity.